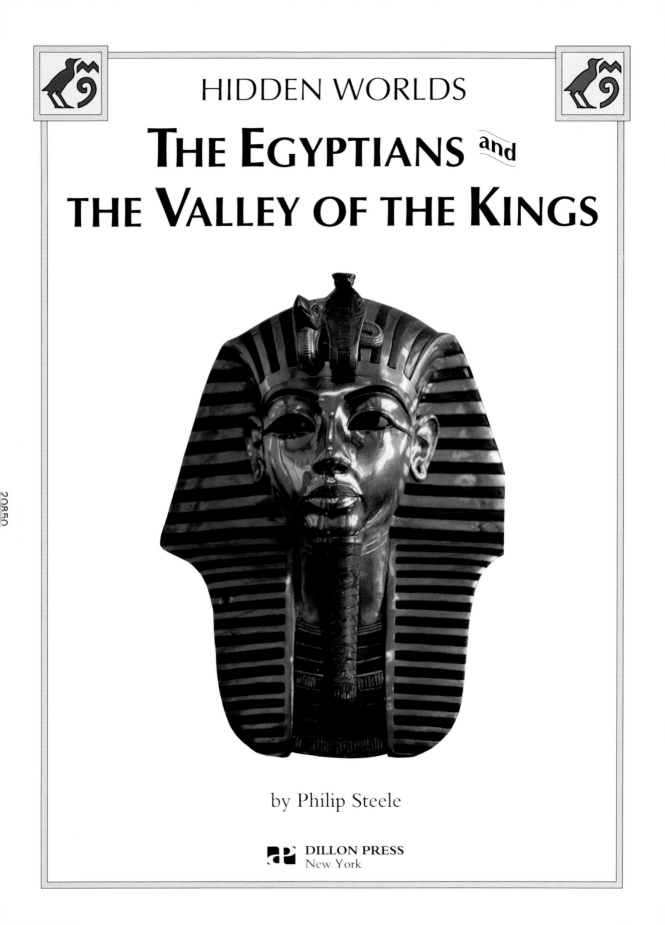

HIDDEN WORLDS

THE EGYPTIANS and
THE VALLEY OF THE KINGS

by Philip Steele

DILLON PRESS
New York

20850

First American publication 1994 by Dillon Press,
Macmillan Publishing Company, 866 Third Avenue,
New York, NY 10022

Macmillan Publishing Company is part of the
Maxwell Communication Group of Companies.

First published in Great Britain
by Zoë Books Limited

A ZOË BOOK

Devised and produced by
Zoë Books Limited
15 Worthy Lane
Winchester
Hampshire SO23 7AB
England

Printed in Italy by Grafedit SpA
Design: Jan Sterling, Sterling Associates
Picture research: Victoria Sturgess
Maps: Gecko Limited
Production: Grahame Griffiths

10 9 8 7 6 5 4 3 2 1

Library of Congress Cataloging-in-Publication Data

Steele, Philip.
  The Egyptians and the Valley of the Kings / by
  Philip Steele.
    p. cm. — (Hidden Worlds)
  A glimpse at Howard Carter's remarkable find of
  Tutankhamun's tomb in Egypt's Valley of the
  Kings
  Includes index.
  ISBN 0-87518-539-8
  1. Valley of the Kings (Egypt)—Juvenile literature.
  2. Egypt—Antiquities—Juvenile literature.
  [1. Valley of the Kings (Egypt) 2. Egypt—
  Antiquities. 3. Egypt—Civilization—To 332 B.C.]
  I. Title. II. Series.
  DT73.B44S73 1994
  932—dc20   93-26311

Photographic acknowledgments
The publishers wish to acknowledge, with thanks, the
following photographic sources:

Ancient Art & Architecture Collection: 4, 9, 10t, 11,
12t, 15b, 18, 19b, 21t, 22, 23b, 24, 25, 26b, 28, 29b;
British Museum: 8t & b, 26t; C. M. Dixon: title page,
15t, 16, 29t; Griffith Institute, Ashmolean Museum,
Oxford: 14t & b, 17, 19t, 21b, 27; Robert Harding
Picture Library / F L Kenett © George Rainbird Ltd:
23t; Manchester Museum, University of Manchester:
20; The Mansell Collection: 10b & 12b; Cass R
Sandak: front cover; Tony Stone Images: 5 & 6.

Contents

The land of the pharaohs

From the air, Egypt seems to be baking in the hot sun. The ground swelters and shimmers. Rocks and sandy deserts stretch east to the Red Sea and west to Libya. There is only one strip of green land to be seen. This long, narrow band of fields and palm trees marks the course of the Nile, one

▲ This royal scepter was held by Tutankhamen, a young pharaoh buried in the Valley of the Kings about 1352 B.C.

▶ In Egypt most of the ancient sites and modern towns are in the valley of the Nile River or in its delta. Empty deserts lie on either side of the river.

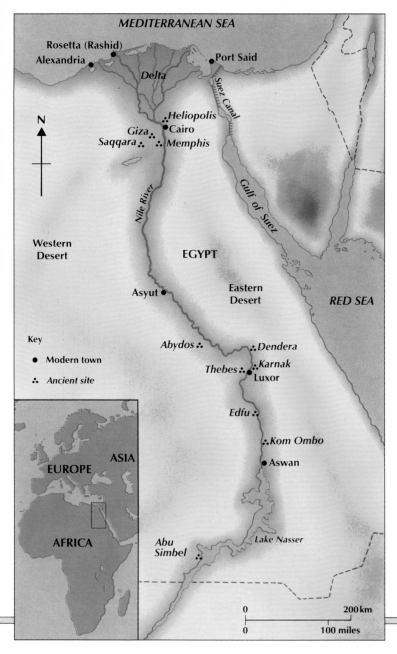

4

of the longest rivers in the world. The Nile River flows northward from central Africa into the Mediterranean Sea. Near the end of its long journey it spills into a maze of waterways, forming a **delta**.

About 8,000 years ago, the people who lived in the Nile Valley started to farm the land. They raised animals and grew crops on the banks of the great river. The soil was good because each year the river flooded and left behind a thick layer of mud.

Over the years, wealthy kingdoms developed in both northern and southern Egypt. The kingdoms joined together in about 3100 B.C., forming a single nation. The kings of ancient Egypt were called **pharaohs**. The pharaohs ruled over a great **empire** that eventually stretched from Syria to the land we now call Sudan.

The Egyptians traded with people in Europe, Asia, and other parts of Africa. They built fine **temples** and cities and invented machines for lifting water, called shadoofs. They observed the stars, wrote down their religious beliefs, painted pictures, and made jewelry of gold and silver.

Royal tombs

Thebes, one of the great cities of ancient Egypt, once stood close to the modern town of Luxor. Scientists who study ancient remains, or **archaeologists**, discovered the site of Thebes and found many tombs, temples, and statues there.

The kings, queens, and priests of Thebes were buried near the west bank of the Nile. Here, there are rocky cliffs and desert valleys called *wadis*. Archaeologists named the burial sites the Valley of the Queens, the Valley of the Nobles, and the Valley of the Kings. Many of Egypt's most famous rulers were buried here secretly, surrounded by gold and other treasures.

▼ The Valley of the Kings is hot and dusty. It lies on the edge of the Western Desert, near the town of Luxor. For thousands of years the valley guarded an ancient secret. Hidden tunnels led down through the rock to the tombs of the ancient pharaohs.

Pyramids and tombs

The Egyptians believed that their rulers were gods. They thought that when a pharaoh died, it was the start of his long journey to the sun. The Egyptians also believed that the gods would only continue to protect the land of Egypt and its new leader if the pharaoh's journey was successful. If he failed it might mean the end of the world. That is why royal burials were believed to be so important.

The early pharaohs lived in northern Egypt. Their first capital city was at Memphis, near modern Cairo. Many pharaohs were buried inside huge stone pyramids, which may still be seen today at Saqqara and Giza. These monuments tower above the skyline, pointing to the sun.

Into the valleys

During the period between 1570 and 1090 B.C., a time in Egypt's history called the New Kingdom, the pharaohs ruled from the south of Egypt, when their capital was at Thebes. The citizens of Thebes built great temples in honor of their dead rulers, but they did not bury them in pyramids. Instead, they hid the pharaohs' tombs in the valleys on the edge of the Western Desert.

The Western Desert

The Egyptians chose to bury their rulers on the west side of the Nile Valley because the sun, to which the dead pharaoh would travel, set over the western hills each night. The Egyptians also believed that people remained in their bodies after death, when they traveled to the other world. The dry desert air made it easier to preserve dead bodies as **mummies**.

Other reasons for building the tombs here were more practical. The rock of the cliffs was

▲ Wooden ships still sail up the Nile past Luxor. To the west, the sun sets over the cliffs and the rocky peak, which houses the Valley of the Kings, one of the most important archaeological sites in the world. Its tombs have shown us how people lived more than 3,000 years ago.

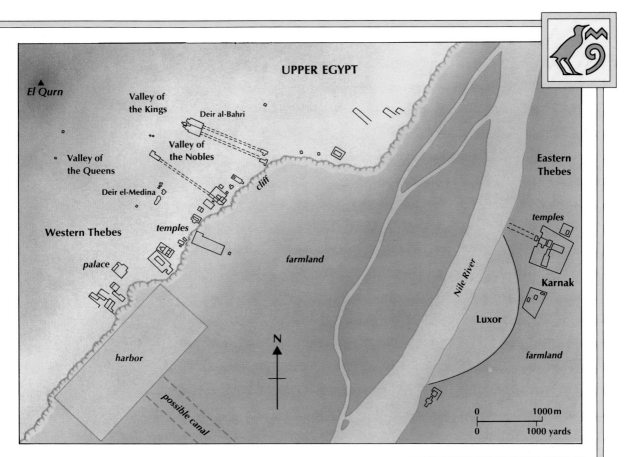

UPPER EGYPT

El Qurn

Valley of
the Kings

Deir al-Bahri

Valley of
the Nobles

Valley of
the Queens

Deir el-Medina

cliff

Western Thebes

temples

palace

harbor

possible canal

farmland

Nile River

Luxor

farmland

Eastern
Thebes

temples

Karnak

N

| 0 | | 1000 m |

| 0 | | 1000 yards |

▲ To the Egyptians it was known simply as "The City." We call it by its Greek name, Thebes. The eastern part of the city lay near the site of modern Luxor. The western part, across the Nile, included canals, royal palaces, temples, and workshops.

▶ Sixty-two tombs have been discovered in the Valley of the Kings, but not all of these belonged to pharaohs. Many other tombs have also been discovered in the nearby Valley of the Queens and Valley of the Nobles.

soft. Passages and chambers could be carved out quite easily. The entrances to the valleys were narrow, so they could be guarded against anyone who would disturb the peace of the tombs. The tombs were always targets for robbers because the pharaohs were buried with all their rich possessions.

The cliffs were also easy to reach. They were only a mile or two from the Nile. During funeral processions priests could walk up into the valleys from the temples of Western Thebes.

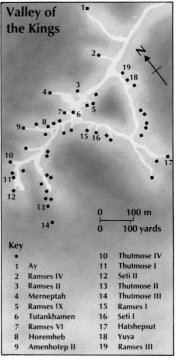

Valley of
the Kings

N

| 0 | | 100 m |

| 0 | | 100 yards |

Key

■			
1	Ay	10	Thutmose IV
2	Ramses IV	11	Thutmose I
3	Ramses II	12	Seti II
4	Merneptah	13	Thutmose II
5	Ramses IX	14	Thutmose III
6	Tutankhamen	15	Ramses I
7	Ramses VI	16	Seti I
8	Horemheb	17	Hatshepsut
9	Amenhotep II	18	Yuya
		19	Ramses III

The search for Thebes

How do scholars find out where to look for ancient sites such as Thebes? There are often clues written down in old **texts**. Some of the pharaohs buried in the Valley of the Kings are known from the stories told about them in the Bible.

In ancient times many Greeks and Romans visited Egypt and wrote about their travels. Diodorus, a Greek from Sicily, visited Thebes and talked to the priests there about the burial of the pharaohs. He wrote a history of the world in about 44 B.C. Strabo, a Greek who later settled in

▲ James Bruce sketched wall paintings in the tomb of the pharaoh Ramses III. When his story was published in 1790, his sketches were made into pictures in the European style. This one showed an ancient Egyptian harpist.

▶ This drawing of the Valley of the Kings was published by Richard Pococke in 1743. It is not very accurate, but it does show the entrance to the valley. The entrance was once hidden by a wall of rock. The boulders have now been cleared away to allow easier access to the valley.

Rome, traveled up the Nile Valley about 20 years later. He wrote about the Valley of the Kings and thought there must be about 40 royal tombs in the cliffs.

Explorers in Egypt

Many hundreds of years after Strabo's time, people read about Thebes in ancient texts and wondered where the city had been built. In 1710 a French priest named Claude Sicard traveled up the Nile. He had read the writings of Diodorus and Strabo and realized that the temples and statues of the Luxor area belonged to ancient Thebes. Sicard **surveyed** and mapped the Valley of the Kings, known locally as Biban el Moluk.

The methods of surveying and mapping used in those days were often inaccurate. Today, archaeologists can survey sites with scientific equipment. They can use aerial photographs to help them make maps. Even so, early maps of the valley give many useful clues.

Other European travelers followed Sicard. An English traveler named Richard Pococke visited the valley in 1739. The Scottish explorer James Bruce came in 1768 on his way to Ethiopia. Both Pococke and Bruce wrote about their travels and published the sketches they had made. Many people in Europe read their books and became fascinated by this distant, dusty valley. It offered them a glimpse of a lost world.

◀ The sun beats down on the bare rocks. The only escape from the sun is underground, in the tombs, where it is cool and shady. A trip to the Valley of the Kings can be very hot and tiring. Explorers who visited the remote valley 250 years ago came on horseback. They also risked being attacked by bandits.

Language detectives

▲ On March 27, 196 B.C., the priests in Memphis recorded their praise for the pharaoh Ptolemy V. The text was written on stone in three ancient scripts. The same stone was found at Rosetta, 2,000 years later.

▼ A young French professor named Jean-François Champollion deciphered the Rosetta Stone in 1822. Decoding ancient scripts can take many years — even in the late 20th century, when scholars are helped by computers.

Two hundred years ago people could read about the city of Thebes in Greek or in Latin, but not in the ancient Egyptian language. There were plenty of examples of ancient Egyptian texts.

Words could be seen everywhere, carved into ancient monuments and painted on walls and pottery. Many were written on **papyrus**, a kind of paper made from reeds. The problem was that the texts were written in a language, or **script**, that nobody could understand.

One script, in use from about 3100 B.C. onward, was made up of little pictures called **hieroglyphs**. Each of these symbols depicted an object, an idea, or a sound.

Another kind of writing, seen from about 1780 B.C. onward, used a more flowing script called **hieratic**. A script called **demotic**, which was easier to jot down quickly, was added about 1,000 years later.

Breakthrough to the past

In 1798 a French army, led by Napoleon Bonaparte, invaded Egypt. Mapmakers, scholars, and artists came with the soldiers. They surveyed and explored the monuments of ancient Egypt. The Valley of the Kings was inspected by a French historian named Vivant Denon. It was later mapped in great detail by Prosper Jollois and Edouard de Villiers.

In August 1799 a French soldier discovered a slab of black stone at Rosetta, in Northern Egypt. On the slab, which became known as the Rosetta Stone, was a piece of text written in three different scripts — hieroglyphic, demotic, and ancient Greek. As ancient Greek could be understood, here, at last, was a key to understanding the mysterious scripts of ancient Egypt. By comparing the scripts, scholars learned how to read ancient Egyptian writing.

A new science came into being — the study of ancient Egypt, called **Egyptology**. Famous Egyptologists included John Gardiner Wilkinson, Karl Richard Lepsius, Auguste Mariette, and Gaston Maspero. During the 1800s and 1900s these scholars came to the Valley of the Kings and translated, or **deciphered**, the hieroglyphs in the tombs.

▼ These hieroglyphs were found in the tomb of Seti I, a pharaoh of the New Kingdom. Scholars found out the names of pharaohs, when they ruled, and many other fascinating details about life in ancient Egypt when they deciphered the ancient texts.

Digging for treasure

► The finest tomb discovered by Giovanni Belzoni was that of the pharaoh Seti I. Its grand burial chamber was decorated with pictures of gods and animals.

▲ Giovanni Belzoni was not only a skilled engineer, but also a showman. He had performed feats of strength on the London stage and appeared in pantomimes. He came to Egypt by way of Spain and Malta.

Today, archaeologists work in a scientific way. Each site is carefully surveyed and mapped. Trenches are dug and soil is removed with painstaking care. Every find is photographed and listed.

The first **excavations** at the Valley of the Kings were carried out with very little care. For many years local people had been digging for any treasures that they could sell. The Europeans who organized digs in the 1800s also removed priceless treasures for personal profit. Valuable finds were lost, stolen, or sold. Monuments were damaged. European tourists camped and lit fires in the tombs. Many remains were shipped out of Egypt and sold to museums in Paris, London, and Berlin.

The most extraordinary treasure hunter was an Italian named Giovanni Battista Belzoni, who arrived in Egypt in 1816. He was a giant of a man, with flaming red hair. Working for the

British **consul** in Cairo, Henry Salt, Belzoni set off for the Valley of the Kings. He crawled into dark passages, battered down doors, and cleared rubble. He made many important discoveries, including the royal tombs of Ay, Ramses I, and Seti I.

Henry Salt sold many of Belzoni's finds to the British Museum. Other finds were put on show at the Egyptian Gallery in Piccadilly, London. People flocked to see the exhibition. It was a public sensation.

Limiting the damage

The archaeologists who visited the Valley of the Kings also made great discoveries, but they, too, were causing damage to the site.

In 1850 the French scholar Auguste Mariette was sent to Cairo. He soon realized that something had to be done to protect the ancient monuments and to keep the national treasures in Egypt. In the following years Mariette set up the Antiquities Service of Egypt, which controlled all the archaeological excavations in Egypt. Mariette and an Englishman, Sir Flinders Petrie, were the first archaeologists in Egypt to work in an organized and responsible way.

▼ The tomb of Seti I is reached by a 320-foot-long passage. This passage has all kinds of false turns, hidden stairs, and deep shafts. It was designed to keep out robbers.

burial chamber

hall

hidden stairs

shaft

entrance corridor

The archaeologists

One by one, the tombs in the Valley of the Kings were surveyed and numbered. They were often cleared too rapidly and the finds were not listed or described properly.

Various methods of excavation were tried. A French archaeologist named Victor Loret dug shafts called **sondages** to see if there were any chambers or passages underground. Other archaeologists dug trenches.

Victor Loret made some great discoveries. One of these was the tomb of Thutmose III. Although this tomb was well hidden in the cliffs, it had been robbed long ago. Finds from the tomb included the remains of a bull that had been killed, jars, jewelry, coffins, food, and model boats. All these had been left for the dead pharaoh for use on his journey to the next world.

In the tomb of Amenhotep II there were mummies from other tombs that had been robbed

▼ These pictures of Egyptian workers were taken by Harry Burton in the early 1900s. Burton was a brilliant English photographer first hired by Theodore M. Davis. He spent 30 years recording the tombs and monuments of ancient Thebes.

in ancient times. They had later been reburied by the priests. Near this tomb, Victor Loret found the fine tomb of Maiherpri, a warrior who was probably a friend of the pharaoh. In his tomb were arrows, quivers, collars for hunting dogs, and a board for playing a game like checkers.

A new series of digs

Between the years 1902 and 1914 an American businessman named Theodore M. Davis **sponsored** a new series of digs in the Valley of the Kings. He was a retired businessman, not an archaeologist, so he needed experts to help him carry out the excavations.

Between 1902 and 1904 Davis worked with a young English archaeologist named Howard Carter. Carter was a skilled artist and naturalist who had already discovered tombs in the region. He had been made Inspector General of Monuments for Upper Egypt when he was only 25 years old.

The teams of archaeologists led by Theodore M. Davis made exciting new finds, including the large tomb of Horemheb, an army general who later became a pharaoh. He had died in about 1320 B.C.

◀ The tomb of Horemheb was discovered by Edward Ayrton in 1908. Its wall paintings were as fresh as the day they were painted, but some of them were not finished.

The mask of Tutankhamen

Were there any more royal tombs to be discovered in the Valley of the Kings? Most people did not think so, but one important clue suggested otherwise. Some pots found in 1908 had been used in preparing the mummy of the young pharaoh Tutankhamen. The tomb of Tutankhamen had never been found — where could it be?

In 1914 a new sponsor took over the valley excavations. Lord Carnarvon was a rich Englishman who had worked with Howard Carter for some years. The outbreak of World War I put a stop to their work, but by 1917 Howard Carter was back in the valley. At last, on November 4, 1922, he made the most famous discovery in the history of archaeology.

The tomb was only a small one, and Tutankhamen had not been a very important pharaoh. What excited Howard Carter was the fact that the ancient **door seals** were still unbroken. Perhaps it had never been disturbed by robbers! Carter made a small hole and peered through, but all he could see was a blocked tunnel. He sent a message to Lord Carnarvon. The sponsor arrived at Luxor with his daughter on November 23. The tomb could now be opened.

▼ Tutankhamen had become ruler at the age of 12, in about 1347 B.C. The head and shoulders of his mummy were covered with a mask of gold. The priests believed that he should be made to look like the Sun God himself.

The treasure store
The door seals were in fact replacements. It was clear that the tomb had been disturbed in ancient times. Even so, it was packed with spectacular treasures. Howard Carter called November 26, 1922, "the day of days, the most wonderful I have ever lived through."

In the gloomy passages and chambers, electric

light now revealed thrones and chairs, carved animals, statues, cups and vases, chests full of jewelry and papyrus, **chariot** wheels, wall paintings, trumpets, fans, and weapons. There was pale ivory, dark ebony, and the dull gleam of gold. Finally, there was a splendid tomb.

For ten years Carter pieced together the story of Tutankhamen. Objects from the tomb were carefully listed and described. It was not always easy. The news of the find traveled fast. Tourists, newspaper reporters, and photographers crowded into the valley from around the world.

◀ Tutankhamen had been buried inside four golden shrines. Each was covered with holy texts and pictures of the gods. When Howard Carter opened the inner shrines, he realized that they had not been disturbed for more than 3,260 years.

The living dead

Archaeologists can find out a great deal from the way in which people were buried.

Normally they find only skeletons, but sometimes bodies are preserved naturally. This has happened in the bogs and marshes of northern Europe and in the deep-frozen soil of Siberia. Bodies buried in dry desert sands are particularly well-preserved. The secret of preparing mummies was also discovered in other desert regions of the world, such as Peru.

The Egyptians were fascinated by death. The west bank of Thebes is sometimes called a **necropolis**. This Greek word means "city of the dead." The Egyptians learned how to prepare mummies as early as 4000 B.C. Preserving dead bodies, or **embalming**, was important to them because they believed that their bodies survived into the next life. The citizens of Thebes even mummified sacred animals such as cats and crocodiles. Poor people were embalmed, but the best treatment was given to those who could pay for it — royalty, nobles, and priests.

Often the brain was the first organ to be removed from the dead body. The heart was left in place, but the kidneys, liver, stomach, and guts were taken out and preserved separately. They were placed in jars in the tomb. The body itself was dried out with a preparation of salty crystals known as **natron**. This process took about 40 days. The body was then stuffed with clay, sawdust, or linen cloth soaked with **resin**. The skin was rubbed with oils, perfumes, and wax. Finally, bandages and cloth were wrapped around the body.

▲ Mummies found in the Valley of the Kings allow us to look at historical figures face to face. This is probably the head of the pharaoh Seti I.

◀ The mummy of Tutankhamen was placed inside three coffins. The outer ones were splendidly decorated with colored glass set in gold. The heavy inner coffin was made of solid gold.

The mummies were placed inside a series of wooden coffin cases. These were shaped like a human body and painted with the face of the dead person. The coffins were then lowered into a stone box called a **sarcophagus**.

Science and superstition

Many of the mummies discovered in the Valley of the Kings were taken to the Cairo Museum and unwrapped in public. They were measured, photographed, and examined by medical experts.

Many people had a superstitious interest in the mummies. Lord Carnarvon died on April 5, 1923, and soon people were saying that he had been "cursed by the mummy of Tutankhamen." They claimed that more than 17 people connected with the excavation had died under strange circumstances.

▶ This wall painting from the tomb of Ramses I explains the importance of royal funerals to the ancient Egyptians. It shows the pharaoh meeting the gods after his death. In order to make sure that this meeting took place, the pharaohs were left with food, weapons, boats, chariots, and clothes for their journey to the next world.

Keys to the past

Howard Carter had set up a site **laboratory**, in the tomb of Seti II. Until 1932, this was where he carried out detailed examination, or **analysis**, of the finds. Further studies were carried out at the Cairo Museum. **X rays** were used to show bones, wounds, and signs of disease or the presence of rings and jewelry under the bandages.

The great age of archaeological discoveries in the Valley of the Kings was now over. However, exciting new scientific discoveries have since given us further information.

Scientific study

Testing of **genes** and **blood groups** has made it easier for scientists to find out which mummies are related to one another. One mummy had been puzzling archaeologists ever since it was found. It was once identified as the pharaoh Akhenaton. However blood tests have since shown that it was probably Tutankhamen's brother, Smenkhkare.

In the late 20th century mummies have been examined with **electron microscopes**. Chemical tests and **radiocarbon dating** have been used to find out when they lived. Chemists have tested paints and the ointments and resins used in embalming to find out what they

▶ A team from Manchester University examines a mummy in 1975. Scientists have found out as much about ancient Egypt as the archaeologists.

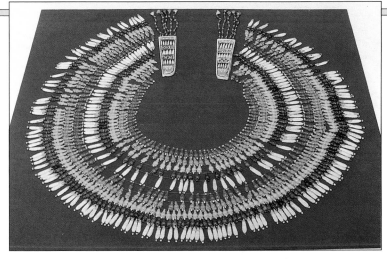

◀ Collars made of cloth, beads, and flowers were found in the Valley of the Kings. They were worn during banquets and included olive leaves, cornflowers, and berries. A flower garland on Tutankhamen's middle coffin included petals of blue lotus, willow, and wild celery.

contained. Analysis of bones has shown that in our world, with its cars and exhaust fumes, lead pollution is 30 times as bad as 3,000 years ago.

Scientists have examined the plants found in the tombs. These included garlands of flowers, bunches of leaves, and reeds and berries. By examining grain, seeds, and tiny samples of pollen they can tell which plants grew in Thebes long ago. Other scientists, called **zoologists**, have examined the various kinds of beetle, mosquito, and louse that have been found in the remains. Some wall paintings show African wildlife such as the ostrich, now found only far to the south.

Geologists have studied the rocks in the Valley of the Kings. They have found out how sudden floods and past excavations have changed the shape of the valley.

◀ These wooden boxes contained food for Tutankhamen to eat on his journey to the other world. Food remains found in the Valley of the Kings included beef, lamb, duck and goose, fruit, beer, and wine.

Rulers and gods

A man could become the next pharaoh by marrying the daughter of the current pharaoh. In certain periods of Egypt's history, the country was ruled by a succession of pharaohs from the same family. Historians call a period of rule by a particular royal family a **dynasty**.

Sometimes the power of the male pharaohs was challenged. Queen Hatshepsut became **regent** when her husband Thutmose II died. She refused to hand over power to his young successor, Thutmose III. When she eventually died, he destroyed many of her statues and removed her name from monuments.

Many symbols of royal power were found in the tombs. There were thrones, crowns decorated with cobras, and false beards made of wood. During his coronation the pharaoh carried a **crook** and **flail**, badges of the god Osiris.

▶ This beautiful scene appears on the golden throne of Tutankhamen. It shows the pharaoh with his queen Ankhesenamen.

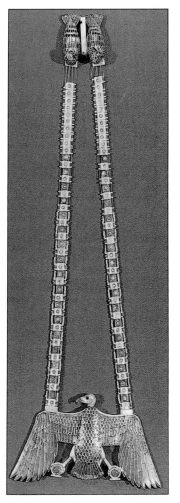

◀ Games called *tjau* and *senet* could be played on this splendid board. They were found in the tomb of Tutankhamen and were made from ebony and ivory. We do not know the rules of the games.

▼ The vulture is one symbol of Nut, the sky-goddess. She was meant to protect Tutankhamen with her broad wings.

Not all life was made up of public ceremonies. The royal court enjoyed feasting, hunting, and playing games. They were entertained by music and dance. The finds in the tombs show that dress, jewelry, and cosmetics were valued by both men and women.

Religious beliefs

The religious life of the pharaohs was important to all Egyptians. Their rulers were in contact with the gods and goddesses who controlled life, death, and the natural world. There was Ra, the sun god and Osiris, the god of death. Isis was the great goddess. Many gods and goddesses were linked to animals. There was Horus the falcon-god, Anubis the jackal, and Sekhmet the lioness who was goddess of war. The chief god of Thebes was Amun, whose symbol was the ram.

The wall paintings in the Valley of the Kings show many of these gods. Seven hundred alone are shown in the tomb of Thutmose III. Spells and prayers written in the royal tombs make up the Book of the Dead, a guide for the journey to the next world.

Builders of the tombs

▲ Some of the most interesting paintings of life in ancient Thebes decorated the tombs of the nobles and royal officials. In the tomb of one, called Smenkhara, the artist has shown how the craftsmen went about their work. There are carpenters, metalworkers, and carvers of the fine white stone called alabaster.

In reality, the survival of ancient Egypt did not depend on the burial of its kings, but on the hard work of its farmers and laborers. How did working people live in ancient Egypt? Wall paintings show us the farmers of the Nile Valley, planting crops, plowing the muddy soil, and counting flocks of geese.

In the tomb of Seti I there were small models of workers carrying hoes, tools, and baskets. There was one for each day of the year, lined up in work gangs with a foreman. A text on each model tells it to carry out any digging work that the pharaoh might need in the other world.

A special workforce
The workers who dug the royal tombs were skilled crafts workers who held important jobs.

They lived in a special village that had been built at Deir el-Medina near the Valley of the Queens in about 1500 B.C. The excavation of this site brought to light fragments of stone and pottery covered with plans and working drawings. There were even funny sketches of other workers. There were delivery notes and details of a **strike**, by the workers.

The ancient tombs were dug from the rocks with spikes, hoes, and mallets made of copper and bronze. Stone chippings were carried out in baskets and dumped on the valley floor. When the passages and chambers had been carved from the rock, the walls were plastered until they were smooth.

Work was carried out throughout the pharaoh's reign. If he died suddenly, the tomb had to be finished in a hurry. The workers, of course, knew every twist and turn of the tomb design. With their secret knowledge of the hidden shafts, stairways, and dead-ends, they probably carried out some of the first tomb robberies.

◀ The ruins of Deir el-Medina today. This walled village housed the work force for the royal tombs. There were between 70 and 120 mud-brick houses in the whole settlement. These workers were much better off than most, but there were still occasional food shortages. The workers rioted in 1153 B.C.

A history of the valley

► The writing on this papyrus tells of tombs being robbed in the Valley of the Kings in 1090 B.C. The problem had become so serious that royal officials were sent to investigate the crimes.

▼ This model boat from the tomb of Tutankhamen reminds us that ancient Egyptians depended on the Nile River for their water, their farming, their trade, and their transportation.

Over the last 400 years the hidden world of ancient Thebes has given up its secrets, one by one. We know now that this city was only a small town during the third century B.C. Its great period of power dated from the beginnings of the

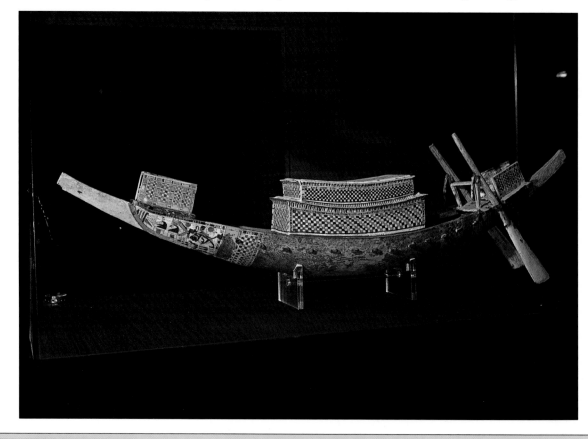

New Kingdom, in about 1570 B.C. When it became the capital of Egypt, the whole country took up the worship of the god of the people of Thebes, called Amun.

The discoveries in the Valley of the Kings have made the eighteenth dynasty, which lasted until 1320 B.C., the best-known period in Egyptian history. This was the age of powerful Queen Hatshepsut and the civilized rule of Amenhotep III.

There were religious troubles at this time. The pharaoh Amenhotep IV, who was married to the beautiful Nefertiti, decided to start a new religion and worship only the sun. He changed his name to Akhenaton. The priests of Amun were horrified. When young Tutankhamen came to the throne, they made sure that he returned to the worship of Amun.

When the pharaoh Horemheb died, rule of the country passed on to his chief official, Ramses I. This was the start of the nineteenth dynasty, which lasted until 1200 B.C. Seti I became pharaoh after Ramses I. Many great buildings and tombs date from the reign of Seti's son, Ramses II, who ruled for 67 years. However this was an age of warfare. There was more trouble in the twentieth dynasty. Fine tombs were still built in the valley, but after 1085 B.C. power returned to Lower Egypt. Amun was still worshiped at Thebes but its days of glory had passed.

Forgotten Thebes

Eventually Egypt was invaded by Persians, Greeks, and Romans. Strangers came to the area around Thebes. Greek and Roman tourists scratched their names on the ancient monuments. Christian monks settled in the western cliffs and the desert. Finally, Arab invaders brought the faith of Islam in A.D. 641. The Valley of the Kings lay unguarded, its tombs looted or blocked by falls of rock.

▲ The jackal god Anubis guarded the entrance to the tomb of Tutankhamen. Why was this ruler buried with so many treasures? They may have been a thanksgiving from the priests of Amun. The priests had held power during the reign of the young pharaoh, and made him bring back the worship of Amun to Thebes.

Past, present, and future

▶ This beautiful head of Tutankhamen is carved from alabaster. It is one of four stoppers made for the pharaoh's burial jars.

The discoveries in the Valley of the Kings have shown that Thebes was home to one of the most advanced civilizations in the ancient world. Many thousands of tourists visit the modern town of Luxor each year to see the great temples of Luxor and Karnak, with their vast pillars and stone avenues.

On the Nile River there are wooden sailing boats as well as cruise ships for tourists. A ferry takes passengers over to the green fields and ditches of the West Bank, with its great statues and temples and its valley tombs.

Conserving the tombs

So many tourists now pass through the Valley of the Kings that their sweat is making the air in the tombs too acid. This is placing the precious wall paintings in danger. Although the archaeological work in the valley is mostly over, **conservation** is still required. Paintings and carvings have to be preserved. The tombs must be kept in a good state of repair. The valley needs to be protected from sudden floods which sometimes rush down the *wadis* of the Western Desert.

Most of the treasures are now kept in museums, but the mummy of Tutankhamen still lies in its sarcophagus in the Valley of the Kings. Was it right for archaeologists to disturb the resting place of the pharaohs? Perhaps so, for in a way they did help the pharaohs become **immortal**. More than 3,000 years after his death, the name Tutankhamen is known around the world.

▲ Not everything has changed on the west bank of the Nile. Beneath the Valley of the Kings, villagers still dig drainage ditches, carry water, and grow crops.

◄ This alabaster cup was found in the tomb of Tutankhamen. Its message reads:
"May your spirit live on,
may you spend millions of
    years,
you who love Thebes,
with your face to the breeze
    from the north
and your eyes seeing
    happiness."

Glossary

analysis: a detailed examination.

archaeologist: someone who studies objects from the past in a careful and scientific manner.

blood group: one of the four main types of blood found in human bodies.

chariot: a vehicle with two wheels, often pulled by a horse.

conservation: preparing or restoring objects to make sure that they stay in good condition.

consul: the representative of a foreign government in a country.

crook: a hooked stick used by a shepherd. In ancient Egypt, this became a symbol of the god Osiris.

decipher: to work out the meaning of a code or an unknown script.

delta: a river may split into several smaller waterways before it enters the sea. This flat, wetland region is called a delta.

demotic: a type of shorthand developed from earlier ancient Egyptian scripts.

door seal: entrances to tombs and some shrines were blocked or tied and stamped with an official seal, which would crack if the tomb was broken into.

dynasty: a series of rulers from the same royal family or the period of their rule.

Egyptology: the scientific study of ancient Egyptian monuments and remains.

electron microscope: a very powerful microscope that uses beams of electrons instead of light. The image is shown on a screen.

embalm: to prepare a dead body for burial with ointments or chemicals.

empire: different countries brought together under a single ruler or government.

excavation: the place where archaeologists dig to find information about the past.

flail: a staff used for threshing or beating grain from the stalk. It was also a symbol of the god Osiris.

gene: part of the chemical code passed on from parents to their children.

geologist: a scientist who studies soil and rock formations.

hieratic: a streamlined version of the hieroglyphic script used in ancient Egypt.

hieroglyph: one of the small picture symbols used to represent words and sounds in ancient Egypt.

immortal:	able to live forever.
laboratory:	a room for carrying out scientific tests.
mummy:	a corpse which has been kept from decay by a process of drying.
natron:	a salty mineral taken from lake beds in ancient Egypt.
necropolis:	a large area given over to burial of the dead or funeral ceremonies.
papyrus:	this kind of reed grows in and around the Nile River. It was used to make a kind of paper. The central part of the stalk was cut into strips and then dried and glued into layers.
pharaoh:	a title given to the kings of ancient Egypt.
radiocarbon dating:	measuring the rate of radioactive decay in an object, in order to date it.
regent:	someone who is appointed to rule if the king or queen is too young or too ill to carry out royal duties.
resin:	the sap that oozes from a pine tree, forming a sticky gum.
sarcophagus:	a large stone container into which the Egyptians placed wooden coffins.
script:	a system of symbols that represent sounds or ideas, such as the letters of the alphabet.
sondage:	a French word meaning "sounding." A shaft, about three feet across, is dug downward in the hope of finding ancient remains.
sponsor:	to put up the money for a project or an expedition.
strike:	the refusal to continue working until the demands of the workforce have been met.
survey:	to make a detailed inspection of a site.
temple:	a large building used for worship.
text:	words that have been written down, as in a book.
wadis:	A desert valley formed by sudden floods. It may remain dry for years on end.
X ray:	an invisible ray that can be used to take photographs of the inside of some objects through the outer covering.
zoologist:	a scientist who studies animals.

Index